the best of grade 5

Piano

Selected and edited by Anthony Williams

FABER *ff* MUSIC

Contents

© 2007 by Faber Music Ltd
This edition first published in 2007
3 Queen Square London WC1N 3AU
Music processed by Graham Pike
Design by Økvik Design
Printed in England by Caligraving Ltd
All rights reserved

ISBN10: 0-571-52775-2
EAN13: 978-0-571-52775-5

To buy Faber Music publications or to find out about the full range of titles available
please contact your local music retailer or Faber Music sales enquiries:

Faber Music Limited, Burnt Mill, Elizabeth Way, Harlow CM20 2HX
Tel: +44 (0)1279 82 89 82   Fax: +44 (0)1279 82 89 83
sales@fabermusic.com   fabermusic.com

Gavotte

from 'French Suite No.5' in G BWV 816/4

Johann Sebastian Bach

An Evening in the Village

from 'Ten Easy Pieces' Sz.39

Béla Bartók

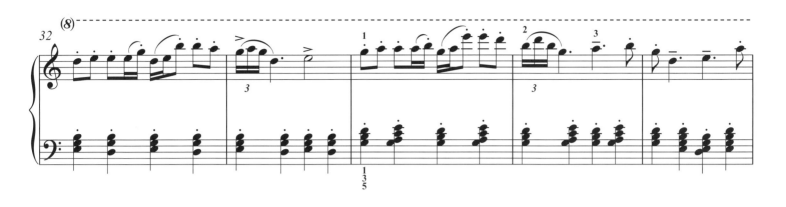

Sonatina in F

Georg Benda

La Tarantelle

from 'Vingt-cinq études faciles et progressives' Op.100

Johann Friedrich Franz Burgmüller

Bossa Nova

from 'Easy Jazzy Piano'

Mike Cornick

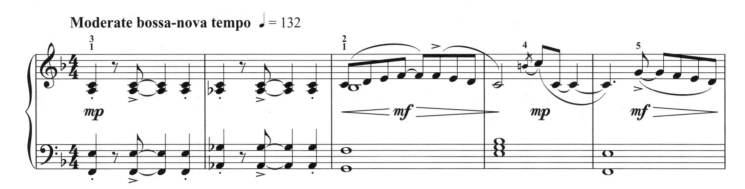

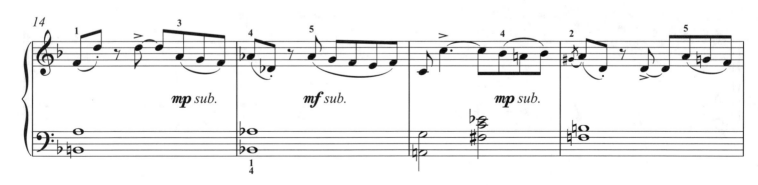

Rondo

Third movement from Sonatina in F, Op.168 No.1

Anton Diabelli

Waltz in D minor

Op.39 No.9

Johannes Brahms

New Orleans Nightfall

from 'New Orleans Jazz Styles'

William Gillock

Tempo I, but with a more pronounced beat

Gigue

Fifth movement from Suite No.7 in G minor, HWV 432

George Frideric Handel

Study in A flat

Op.47, No.23

Stephen Heller

Tomorrow

Peter Jarrett

Novelette

from 'Twenty-four Easy Pieces' Op.39

Dmitri Kabalevsky

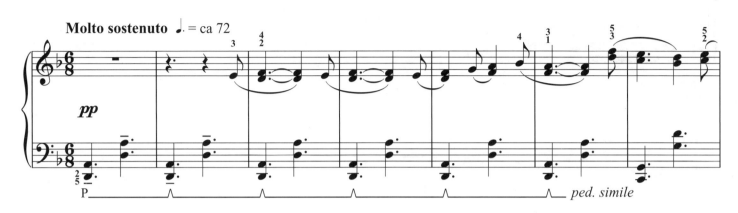

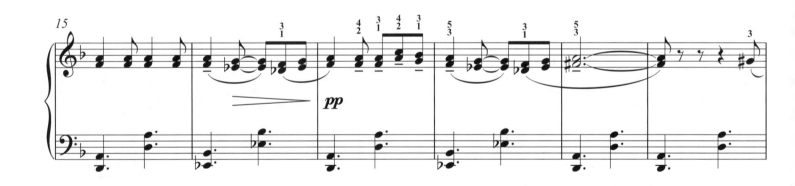

Allegro molto

First movement from Sonatina in F Op.88 No.4

Friedrich Kuhlau

Pajaro Triste

from 'Impresiones intimas'

Federico Mompou

Allegro moderato in F

Leopold Mozart

Prelude in D minor

Op.40 No.3

Anatol Konstantinovich Lyadov